Beginners' Programme
to
Piano & Synthesizer
(Prelude)

Beginners' Programme
to
Piano & Synthesizer
(Prelude)

By

Nitin Srivastava

(Guitarmonk)

UNICORN BOOKS

Publishers
UNICORN BOOKS
F-2/16, Ansari Road, Daryaganj, New Delhi-110002
☎ 23275434, 23262683, 23262783 • Fax: 011-23257790
E-mail: info@unicornbooks.in • *Website:* www.unicornbooks.in

Distributors
Pustak Mahal®
J-3/16, Daryaganj, New Delhi-110002
☎ 23276539, 23272783, 23272784 • Fax: 011-23260518
E-mail: info@pustakmahal.com • *Website:* www.pustakmahal.com

Sales Centres

- 10-B, Netaji Subhash Marg, Daryaganj, New Delhi-110002
  ☎ 23268292, 23268293, 23279900 • Fax: 011-23280567
  E-mail: salespmahal@airtelmail.in, rapidexdelhi@indiatimes.com
- 6686, Khari Baoli, Delhi-110006
  ☎ 23944314, 23911979
- Bengaluru: ☎ 080-22234025 • Telefax: 080-22240209
  E-mail: pustak@airtelmail.in • pustak@sancharnet.in
- Mumbai: ☎ 022-22010941, 022-22053387
  E-mail: rapidex@bom5.vsnl.net.in
- Patna: ☎ 0612-3294193 • Telefax: 0612-2302719
  E-mail: rapidexptn@rediffmail.com
- Hyderabad: Telefax: 040-24737290
  E-mail: pustakmahalhyd@yahoo.co.in

ISBN 978-81-7806-225-9

Edition: January, 2011

Printed at : Param Offsetters, Okhla, New Delhi-110020

Preface

I have great pleasure to bring forth this book as part of my endeavour to give some sort of organisation and structure to the music education in India.

Going by my professional experience in the last two decades, I have realized that India badly needs an organized music teaching system. The non-existence of such a system is one of the factors that plagues music education in our country. Non-compulsory music education and lack of awareness are the other factors which add to its present state.

This is the first book of the four volume book series published under the same title. As there is a dearth of constructive content for study and reference on this subject, to a great extent, this book will serve the purpose. The well organized content and the exercises of this book are a first-class study material for the aspiring students of music to prepare for various examinations. Even a 5 year old learner can use this book and it will help him to achieve the desired goal in a short span of time.

It is a matter of great pride and pleasure to note that my other books on music are well received by students and readers alike across the globe. They are also introduced as text books in many schools. We reach out all the places and regions through these books and thus we would be able to serve you without our physical presence.

I thank readers, students and others for their support and patronage. Your suggestions and comments on the further improvement of this book will be thankfully acknowledged and the same will be incorporated in the next edition.

Author

Overview

THE OBJECTIVES

The primary objective of this book is to familiarise the learners with terminologies, exercises and repertoires along with the audios of the compositions. This would help the learners to get a clear perspective on various aspects of the subject.

WHOM IS THIS BOOK FOR?

The book is for complete beginners who know nothing about the instrument, the students who prepare for examinations and the teachers who train the students.

THE SPECIAL FEATURES

- It is customized into levels and can be covered very easily in 12-24 sessions maximum based on time involvement.
- It is an ideal book for teachers who help their student in constructive sessions and productive outcome.
- The book is a step-by-step guide which takes a student from one level to the next. It also inspires success at every grade via achievements which motivates students to get curious and interested in further learning.
- This book contains an audio-CD that instructs on speed and movement of tune: and it is a good reference for the learners who find difficulties in staff reading.
- It contains the basics of staff notations which is very useful information for any music beginner.
- It is a compilation of very significant compositions, rated at a global standard, essential for any music student.

- It offers finger movements which are the most important part for a quality and right learning and support to both teacher and student.
- It offers exercise, pop music repertoire, music theory and Practice Compositions

HOW WILL THIS BOOK HELP YOU?

- It can help you in going about a step-by-step and systematic learning
- A quality and constructive repertoire of songs for your personal performance.
- It instructs you on finger patterns, so as to help both teacher and student with accurate fingering.
- You can expect a basic performance from yourself and can render a medley of tunes on any platform after practicing the given tunes.
- It can assist you, to a great extent, for a performance preparation and content and, thus, it can bring out a musician in you.

Content

Indian Songs Repertoire

WHAT IS KEYBOARD?

A keyboard is an instrument that is played by pressing keys that cause hammers to strike tuned strings and produce sounds

TYPES OF KEYBOARD AND ITS ARCHITECTURE:

- **ACOUSTIC KEYBOARD (a.k.a Piano)**

Acoustic means *non-electric*, each key on an acoustic keyboard connects to a string, on pressing the key; it triggers to the string corresponding to that key and then string begins to vibrate very fast.

To curb the vibrations that get produced by pressing the key, we usually have soft cloth like material that resides over the strings inside the keyboard.

Grand Piano: This Piano has got a lid which can be kept opened with the help of a stick that comes with the piano. Playing a Piano with the Lid opened gives a more deep tone.

Upright Piano: it has also been called as Vertical because in it, the strings are vertical.

PIANO PEDALS

Modern pianos usually have three pedals as:

- **Damper Pedal** (Sustain): It is the right pedal which is used to sustain the sound until we release the pedal.
- **Middle Pedal** (Sostenuto): It is used to sustain selected note or group of notes, while playing other notes normally.
- **Soft Pedal:** It is the left pedal used to create a softer sound.

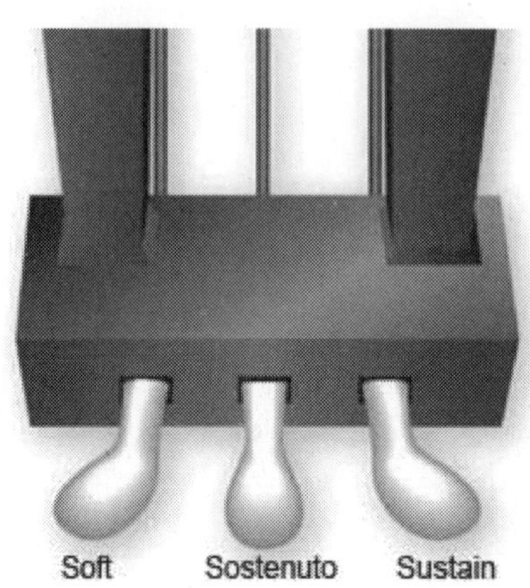

- **ELECTRONIC KEYBOARD (SYNTHESIZERS)**

Synthesizer is an electronic keyboard that generally uses oscillator which produces a sound. The electronic sound gets manipulated by knobs, buttons which changes the shape of the sound's waveform.

Electronic keyboards are available in a wide variety of shapes, sizes, colors, brands and price ranges. The most popular brands in electronic keyboards are Yamaha, Korg, Roland, Casio etc. As the term 'electronic' conveys, they are played using electricity.

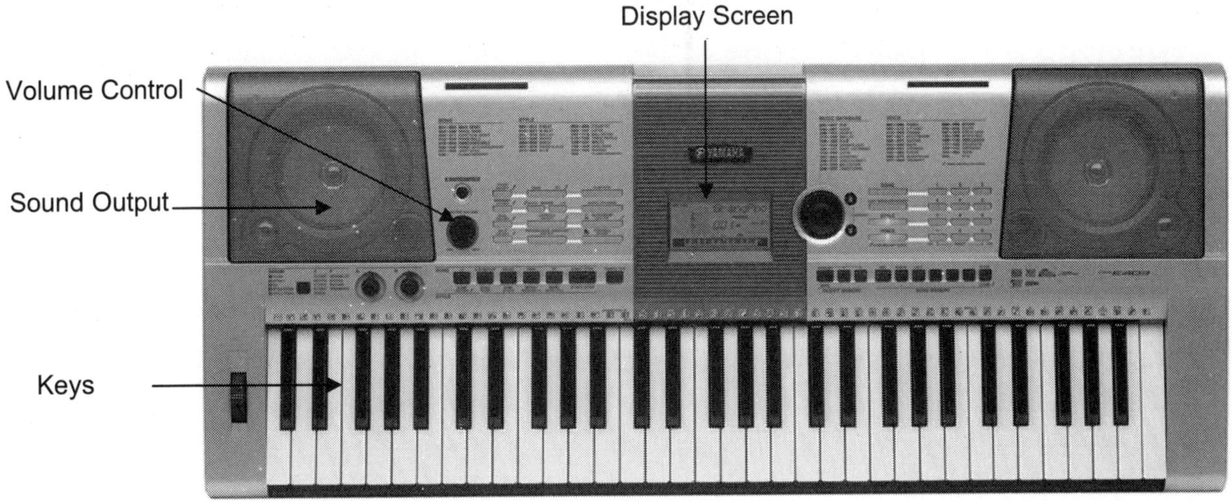

A standard professional keyboard usually comes in 5 octave range having standard piano size keys, and is generally recommended to all beginners. Considering the price, budget and a beginners' perplexity about music, it is even good to start after learning with small size keyboards particularly in case of kids less than 5 years.

There are differences to use a small size and a professional size keyboard which can be guided by the teacher. The electronic keyboards make it very easy to create music and as being electronic, they also have numerous other features, particularly with regard to recording, tutorial and the like. The other advantages are various tones & sounds (of different music instruments), rhythm styles metronome etc. All these features help tremendously to explore music learning in a better and effective manner. Most of these keyboards can also be connected to a computer for performing multimedia activities.

PIANO MAINTENANCE TIPS

- Tune your piano regularly.
- Don't put a piano next to a frequently opened outside door, near heating ducts, against direct sunlight,. humidity and sudden changes in temperature.

- For cleaning, use a feather duster rather than a cloth so as to avoid the rasping effect of dust.
- The piano lid should be closed only when necessary and while the lid provides protection when the piano is not in use, it can also lead to yellowing of the white keys.
- Bug sprays and mothballs should not be used for inside of the piano nor do try to oil it yourself.
- Many problems can be prevented by playing your piano frequently. These include the accumulation of dust and rust.

SYNTHESIZER MAINTENANCE TIPS

- Read the instructions carefully from the manual before using the instrument.
- Always plug and unplug the adaptor gently.
- Don't use the power chord with wet hands.
- Gently handle the keys and control-buttons of your instrument.
- Do replace all the batteries at the same time.
- Do not keep your instrument to direct sun light, extreme temperature, humid dusty places.
- Keep the instrument out of the reach of small children.
- Protect your instrument from any type of liquid substance.

Keyboard Stand

Keyboard Stands comes in variety of designs, functionality and is indispensable for security and right posture.

All Keyboard stands are adjustable in heights.

Sitting Stool

SITTING POSTURE

- You should be comfortable and relaxed at all time while playing piano.
- Bench or stool should have a comfortable distance with the keyboard.
- The keys should be at an appropriate height so that hands and forearms should be parallel to the ground.
- Try to keep your elbows and shoulders relaxed and use your arm muscles to initiate movements.
- Your feet should rest confidently on the floor.
- Your neck should be straight.
- Your hands should have a relaxed curve over the keys.
- Your back should be straight and you are not sprawling.

Note: You should not experience pain while playing. If you do, take a break, find a more comfortable position, and consult a doctor if the pain persists.

FINGERS

Always look for an optimized way of playing while planning to play any composition and for that we need to have an optimized way of how to use the fingers and using the best finger to play each note is a very important. And for that imagine your fingers being numbered 1 through 5 with thumb as number 1 and moving towards the little finger as number 5 *(as shown below)*.

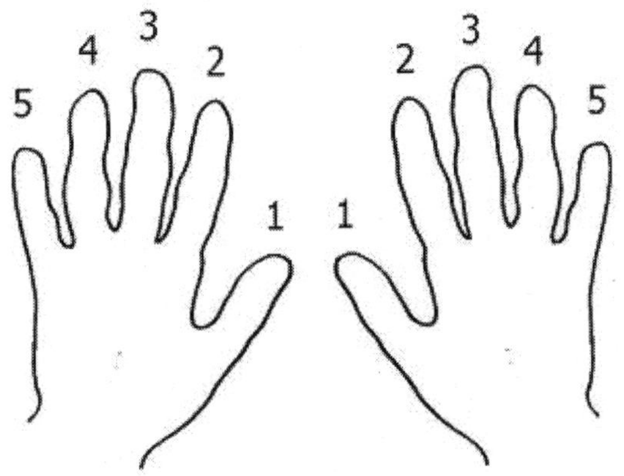

HOW TO CURVE THE FINGERS?

While placing your hands on the keys, keep your hands arched and fingers slightly curved so as to avoid being cramped and tired *(as shown in the picture under the section 'Sitting Posture' above).*

HOW TO RECOGNIZE NOTE NAMES:

Each key on the keyboard represents a definite musical note having names ranging from A to G (A, B, C, D, E, F, and G).
The seven notes names (A, B, C, D, E, F, and G) are all on the white keys. We use the same white keys naming with some added symbol to name the black keys.

If you will observe from the top view of the keyboard you will observe a fixed pattern being repeated in the form of two black keys and then three black keys, this way the black keys appears in consecutive groups of two and three as shown.

FINDING THE C, F ON PIANO

Ad discussed above, keyboard can be seen in pair of 2 and 3 black keys as 2 – 3 – 2 – 3– 2 – 3 ...and on. Imagine 2 black Keys as Chopsticks and 3 Black Keys as Fork (A very traditional and peppy way to remember C & F notes)

Now Just Remember that Chopstick will start with the letter **C** and Fork starts with the letter **F**

- The White Key to the left of the chopsticks is the note **C**.
- The White Key to the left of the fork is the note **F**.

As there are only 7 Alphabets used in music i.e. from A to G (A, B, C, D, E, F & G), if you move from C you have the notes D, E, F, and G. After **G,** you will start from **A** again ***(as there is no 'H' in Music)***.

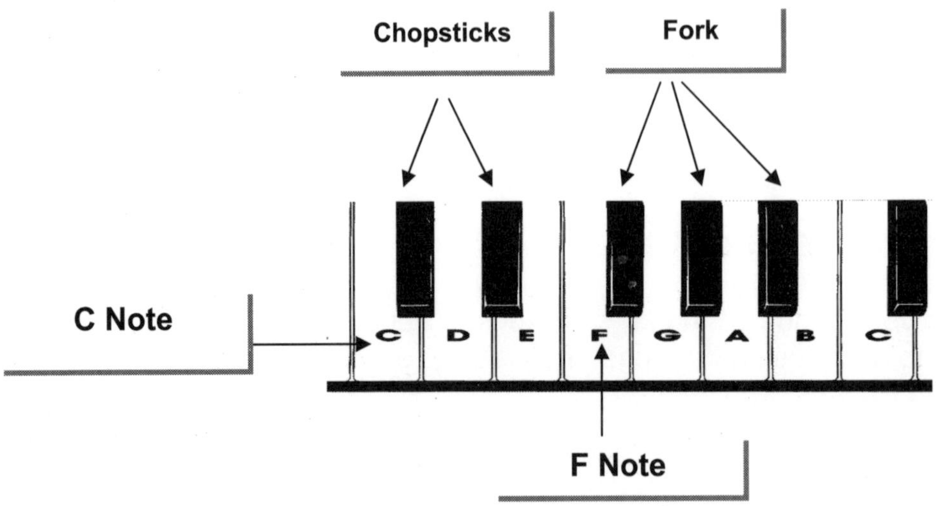

DEFINITIONS AND TERMINOLOGIES

- **Note:** A note is a name given to describe a particular music frequency or pitch. There are 12 notes in music describe with the help of 7 names as:-

  A B C D E F G

  The remaining 5 notes are defined by using Sharp or Flat symbols.

  So there are total 12 notes in music as:
  A, A#/Bb, B, C, C#/Db, D, D#/Eb, E, F, F#/Gb, G, G#/Ab

- **Interval:** An interval refers to distance (musical distance) between any two notes. The two most important intervals are *half tone* (least music interval) and *whole tone* (equals 2 half tones).

- **Scale:** The word Scale derived from the Latin word 'Scale' meaning ladder. So just like a ladder. Scale is a series of steps of notes that can be taken in ascending and descending order.

- **Sharp:** A Sharp symbol ***(#)*** raises the frequency of a note by halftone/semitone. The suffice sharp is used for a black key to the right of (or higher than) white key.

- **Flat:** A Flat symbol ***(b)*** decreases the frequency of a note by halftone/semitone. The suffice flat is used for a black key to the left of (or lower than) a white key.

- **Tempo:** It defines the speed of beat per minute.

- **Chords:** A combination of three or more notes played simultaneously. In layman terms, chords are the part of music being played at the background i.e. over the melody line, as the background music.
  - Chords can be classified into two main categories: -
    - 1) Major chords also known as *Primary Chords*
    - 2) Minor chords also known as *Secondary Chords*

- **Octave**: It is the eighth tone above a given pitch having twice as many vibrations per second. It can also be the eighth tone below a given pitch with half as many vibrations per second.

- **Staff:** Staff consists of five horizontal lines parallel to each other having four spaces. Plenty of symbols are placed over it to express the music. Appropriate music symbols, depending upon the intended effect, are placed on the staff according to their corresponding pitch or function.

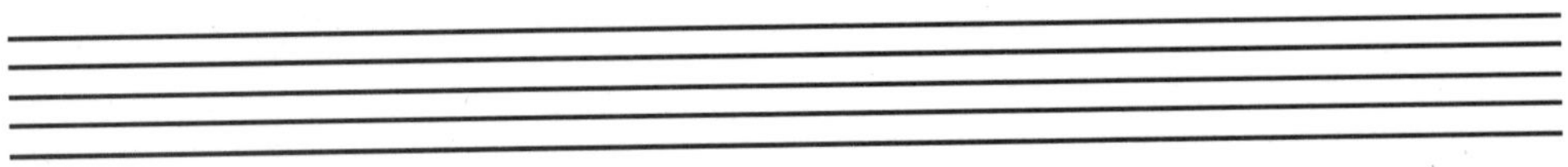

- **Lines and Spaces:** The lines and spaces are numbered from bottom to top; the bottom line is the first line and the top line is the fifth line.

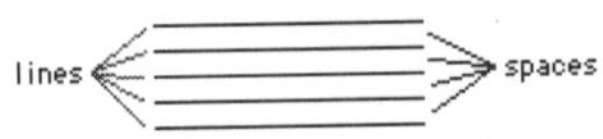

- **Clef:** A symbol placed at the beginning of the staff that indicates and fixes the pitch of the notes over the staff.

- **Treble Clef (or G clef):** Generally, the treble clef signals notes to be played by the right hand and this clef is also called the G clef as shown.

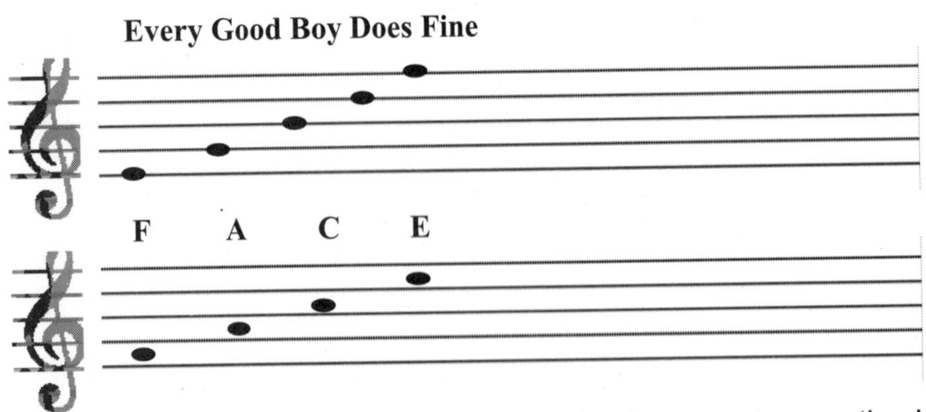

- **Bass Clef (or F clef):** Your left hand plays the lower notes on the keyboard, which are also called bass notes and the clef representing them is called as Bass Clef or F clef.

- **Note Value:** A note value indicates the relative duration of a note, using the color or shape of the note head, the presence or absence of a stem, and the presence or absence of flags/beams.

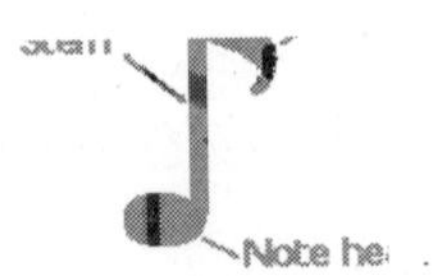

- When a **stem** is present, it can go either up (from the right side of the note head) or down (from the left side). In most cases, the stem goes down if the note-head is on the center line or above, and up otherwise. Any flags/tail always goes to the right of the stem.

- **Beams:** When two or more notes which would normally have flags (eighth notes or shorter) appear successively, the flags may be replaced by beams as shown:

♪ ♪ = ♫

Name	***Note***	**Rests**
Whole Note *or* Semibreve	𝅝	𝄻
Half Note *or* Minim	𝅗𝅥	𝄼
Quarter Note *or* Crochet	♩	𝄽
Eighth Note *or* Quaver	♪	𝄾
Sixteenth Note *or* Semiquaver	𝅘𝅥𝅯	𝄿

- **Measures/Bars:** Grouping of the beats into small batches till the bar ends. Each measure has a specific number of beats depending upon the composer's feel behind the melody.

- **Barline:** Differentiating each measure (containing beats) with a vertical line is called *Barline* as shown:

- **Single Barline:** Go on to the single measure.

- **Double Barline:** Go on to the next section of the song, which will have a change, whether it's a new tempo, new grouping of beats per measure?

- **Repeat (one thin and one thick Barline, plus two dots):** Repeat the music from the beginning of the song.

- **End (one thin and one thick Barline):** Reached at the end of the song.

- **Time Signature:** Expresses the number of beats and nature of note to be used in a bar. It is expressed in fraction form wherein the top number shows how many beats there will be in a bar and the bottom number shows what kind of beats they will be.

- **Key Signature:** The sharps or flats symbols placed at the beginning of the staff.

- **Ledger lines:** Short lines placed above and below the staff to reach the pitches of the composition that are beyond the range of staff.

- **Staccato –** It is indicated by a dot over or under a note, means shortening of a note.

- **Da Capo (D.C.)** – To repeat from a composition from the beginning.

- **Da Capo al fine (D.C. al fine)**: To repeat from the beginning up to the word ***fine***.

- **Dal Segno (D.S.):** To repeat from the sign ***$.***

WHY MUSIC

Music learning enhances several qualities in the learners such as problem solving, teamwork, goal setting, self-expression, coordination, memory skills, self-confidence, esteem, concentration and poise. Music learning also improves organizational skills as how to organize tasks and time-management etc.

The benefits of learning music can be seen in one's personal as well as professional life. These benefits can be classified into four categories as given below.

Physiological as coordination between mind and muscles, hands-eye coordination, development of fine motor skills

Mental Benefits

Encourages creativity, concentration and focus, use of left and right brain, intellectual stimulation, self-control

Emotional Benefits

Aesthetic appreciation, emotional expression, self-confidence, feeling of accomplishment, spiritual experience

Social Benefits

Shared activity and communication, performing for an audience, music is an international language, a sense of pride and accomplishment

Effects of Music on Brain

Several studies have been conducted about effects of music on one's brain. Scientists have observed that children who are exposed to music or who plays a musical instrument perform better in academics than other students who don't participate in musical activity. Music learning helps in IQ, vocabulary and development of certain parts of brain.

The very best engineers and technical designers in the Silicon Valley industry are, nearly without exception, practising musicians. Music training can enhance brain functions.

A research team exploring the link between music and intelligence reported that music training is far superior to computer instruction in dramatically enhancing children's abstract reasoning skills, the skills necessary for learning math and science.

The musician is constantly adjusting decisions on tempo, tone, style, rhythm, phrasing, and feeling, training the brain to become incredibly good at organizing and conducting numerous activities at once.

THE POWER OF MUSIC

The man that hath no music in himself, Nor is not moved with concord of sweet sounds, is fit for treasons, stratagems and spoils.

—William Shakespeare

MUSIC THERAPY

Scientific studies have attempted to measure the potential benefits of music and have found:

- Music has a beneficial effect on our physiological functions, slowing the pulse and heart rate, lowering blood pressure, and decreasing the levels of stress hormones.
- Music's form and structure can bring order, encouraging coordination and communication
- Not only reduces stress, anxiety but also helps relieve depression and increase self-esteem.
- Reduce burnout and improves mood
- Significantly reduces emotional distress and boosts quality of life
- Music is a significant mood-changer and reliever of stress.

"The soothing power of music is well-established, and has been used for hundreds of years to treat illnesses and restore harmony between mind and body. It has a unique link to our emotions, thus being an extremely effective stress management tool."

"Play a tune on the guitar and sing along. That works even in the worst of times. By the time I'm done with the song, I've breathed deep, I've controlled myself to some degree to be able to sing on key :-), and I've come back into myself, and more into the real time moment." – Anonymous

Facts about Corporate Stress

- Average 12.8 million working days are lost to stress, depression and anxiety and approximately 5 million people in the UK feel "very" or "extremely" stressed by their work. One can conclude that how big this loss is to the ideal productivity.
- The Confederation of British Industry estimates businesses lost £10.2 billion average per year through lost productivity caused by stress.
- Research from Harvard University observes that work stress is as harmful to health as smoking or taking no exercise.
- According to the American Academy of Family Physicians, two-thirds of office visits to family doctors are for stress-related symptoms.
- Almost everyone experiences events that they find difficult to cope with. In a recent poll, 89 per cent of people said they had experienced serious stress in their lives.

- Stress-related mental disorders have been called the fastest-growing occupational (work-related) disease in the U.S.
- Your health is in your hands. Far-sighted employers now provide their employees with tools to manage stress - from paying for therapists to visit their premises offering onsite massage and other powerful holistic treatments to arranging seminars to educate their employees to manage stress effectively. (Source: Worldwide web)

Benefits of Corporate Music Workshop

- Improved Employee Engagement
- Reduced Absenteeism
- Enhanced Customer Service
- Improved Performance
- Reduced Attrition
- Enhanced Quality of Work
- Improved Team Interaction

Some Music Cure

The classical compositions (ragas) of music create deep impact on our mind and emotions.

Diseases	*Relative Ragas*
• Insomnia (sleeplessness)	Puriya
• Asthma, chronic cold, cough, tuberculosis, Sinus and chest related problems	Bhairavi
• Anger, mental instability	Malhar
• Impurities of blood an	Asavari
• d relative diseases	
• Mental disorders and impatience	Saurat & Jaijaivanti
• Mental concentration, liver ailments	Hindola

Anti-Stress Music Album: Guitarmonk has produced series of Raga-Based Albums name as **'Kayotsarg'** and they are used as an anti-stress tool at many corporate companies. For information about licenses, albums please email at guitarmonk.info@gmail.com

MUSIC IN SCHOOLS

The existing music education system of schools in India has several limitations:

- Music objectives, curricula, benefits are not clearly defined; music is just for the sake of formality without anyone owning responsibility to it.
- Musical intelligence/understanding is terribly missing in majority of schools which is directly and indirectly affecting the students' personality growth.
- Lack of standardized curriculums and organized/trained teachers who are able to cater international and general parameters.
- Music is not considered as a core academic subject but a part-time activity
- Lack of standardized university level system to train teachers to impart quality music education.
- School kids learn music outside the school premises
- School music education is only limited to 2 to10 percent kids who are good at music. In some schools sports are so dominant that music is taken disrespectfully and by granted.
- Most prodigies miss their school support in catering their interest and talent.
- Absence of basic philosophy and guide which should direct the music programme..

Objectives of Music Education

- To imbibe in them a complete personality growth at a realistic level.
- To relate music learning with visible & practical benefits in students' personality at every level of education and contribute its benefits in overall sphere of their life as academic education, society, family, emotional well being, aesthetical appreciation, friendly and loving environment.
- To cover the core competency skills and standardized concepts at different levels of education
- To let them perform individually and as a group (ensembles)
- To demonstrate music learning through positive attitudes, skills and lifelong learning to occur in every sphere of academics, social and spiritual growth.

COMPOSITIONS

(A collection of special practice repertoire...)

Ainsi Font, Font, Font

Beginner's Keyboard Certification

Pianomonk

Alouette

Beginner's Keyboard Certification

Pianomonk

Amazing Grace

Beginner's Keyboard Certification

Pianomonk

Brother John Sing & Play

Beginner's Keyboard Certification

Pianomonk

Clementine

Beginner's Keyboard Certification

Pianomonk

For Health and Strength

Beginner's Keyboard Certification

Pianomonk

Jingle Bells

Beginner's Keyboard Certification

Pianomonk

London Bridge

Beginner's Keyboard Certification

Pianomonk

Old MacDonald Had a Farm

Beginner's Keyboard Certification

Pianomonk

Twinkle, Twinkle Little Star

Beginner's Keyboard Certification

Pianomonk

Are You Sleeping?

Beginner's Keyboard Certification

Pianomonk

For Health and Strength

Beginner's Keyboard Certification

Pianomonk

INDIAN Pop Songs

MUSIC CHORDS AND LYRICS

(A beautiful repertoire for all music lovers and students ...)

INDIAN SONGS

1. Dooba Dooba
2. Boondein
3. Pal
4. Yaaron
5. Tere Bin Jina Nahin
6. O Sanam
7. Ye Hawa Kehti Hain Kya
8. Purani Jeans

DOOBA DOOBA REHTA HOON

1

Artist: Mohit Chauhan
Album: Boondein
Scale: F Major

```
F                                     Bb          F
(Dooba Dooba rehta hoon aankhon me teri,
F                                    Bb              F
Deewana ban gaya hoon main chaahat me teri),              X 2
         Dm         C               Dm       C
Ab din guzarte nahin, ratein kat-ti nahin,
      Dm     C          Dm     C                    F
Teri tasvir se baat ban-ti nahin..hoooo Aa-ja

Am                 F
(Koi jaane na, pehchaane na
    Dm         Bb              G                        C          C7
Yeh hua kaise, tum aagaye khwabon mein aise)               X 2
Dm    C          Dm     C  Bb       C       F
Bewafa, sun oh bewafa, bewafaa, na jaa

F                                      Bb         F
(Dooba Dooba rehta hoon aankhon me teri)

Am                     F                      Dm                       Bb
(Tum jo mil gaye, deeye jal gaye, mere khwabon mein
           G                         C    C7
Ban jao tum mere humsafar,)                            X 2
Dm   C           Dm    C  Bb     C          F
Bewafa, sun oh bewafa, bewafaa, na jaa

F                                   Bb         F
(Dooba Dooba rehta hoon aankhon me teri,
F                                     Bb              F
Deewana ban gaya hoon main chaahat me teri),                         X 2
         Dm         C               Dm       C
Ab din guzarte nahin, ratein kat-ti nahin,
      Dm     C          Dm     C                    F
Teri tasvir se baat ban-ti nahin..hoooo Aa-ja
                  Dm    C         Dm     C           Bb   C       F
Na ja bewafa, bewafa, na jaa, bewafa, aa ja, bewafa,  na jaa
F                 Bb     F
La la la la, le aa, la l la, l l
```

Dooba Dooba Rehta hoon,

Ankhon mein teri,

Deewana ban gaya hoo main,

Chaahat mein teri,

Ab din gujarte nahi,

Ratein kat-ti nahin,

Teri tasveer se,

Baat banti nahi,

Ho...aa jaa..

BOONDEIN

2

Artist: Mohit Chauhan
Album: Boondein
Scale: F Major

```
F        F
Koi ho, yaadon mein,
Am                  Bb
Palko pe boondein liye,
Gm         C
Aaeina bani,
     Bb          C
Yeh aankhen teri

F            F
Dheemi si, khusbu hai
Am                       Bb
Haawao ke jhokon ne jo,
Gm        C
Chuke tujhe,
Bb        C
Churaaayeee

F             F
Saanson ki, raahon mein,
Am                      C7
Kya mile sakenge kabhi,
Gm             C
Dhoonde tujhe,
Bb         C
Nigahe meri

F            F
Hoton se, hole se,
Am                   Bb
Sargam jo bahne lagi,
Gm      C
Aane lagi,
Bb        C
Chahe meri

F              F
Saathi the, janmo se,
Am                        Bb
Rahon mein kyu kho gaye,

Gm            C
Manzil humein,
Bb         C
Bulane lagi,
F
Hey hey e e he he,

F             F
Nagma ho, bhiga sa
Am                   Bb
Ya tum ho koi gazal,
Gm      C
Har pal jise
Bb          C
Gungunata rahu

F                     Bb F
Hey hey e e he he,
F                         Bb C
Hey, hey a ha ha
```

Koi ho,

Yaadon mein,

Palko pe boondein liye,

Aaeina bani,

Yeh Aankhen Teri,

Dheemi si,

Khushbu hai,

Haawao ke jhonko ne jo,

Chuke tujhe,

Churaayee...

Saanson ki,

Rahon mein,

Kya milk sakenge kabhi,

Dhoonde tujhe,

Nigahe meri,

PAL

3

Artist: K.K.
Album: Pal
Scale: E Major

E F#m A B
(Hum rahe ya na rahe kal, kal yaad aayenge yeh pal)

E F#m
Pal, yeh hain pyaar ke pal,
A B
Chal, aa mere sang chal
C#m G#m
Chal, soche kya
F#m B
Chhoti si hai zindagi
C#m G#m F#m B
Kal mil jaaye to hogi khushnaseebi
E F#m B E
Hum rahe ya Na rahe, yaad aayenge yeh pal) – 2

G#m A G#m A
Shaam ka aanchal odhke aayi
F#m B
Dekho voh raat suhaani
G#m A G#m A
Aa likh de hum dono milke
F#m B
Apni yeh prem kahaani

E F#m B E
Hum rahe ya na rahe, yaad aayenge yeh pal)

G#m A G#m A
Aane waali subha jaane
F#m B
Rang kya laaye deewaani
G#m A G#m A
Meri chaahat ko rakh lena
F#m B
Jaise koi nishaani

E F#m B E
Hum rahe ya na rahe, yaad aayenge yeh pal)

Hum Rahe ya na rahe kal,

Kal yaad aayenge yeh pal,

Pal, Yeh hai pyaar ke pal,

chal aa mere sang chal,

Chal, soche kya,

Chhoti si hai zindagi,

Kal mil jaaye to hogi,

Khushnaseebi,

Hum rahe ya Na rahe, yaad,

aayenge yeh pal....

YAARON

4

F   Bb F
Yaaron dosti badi hi haseen hai,
        Dm   Gm   Bb   F
Yeh na ho to kya phir, bolo yeh zindagi hai,
    BbM7   F   F   Bb
Koi to ho raazdaar, be garaj tera ho yaar,
     F   BbM7
Koi to ho raazdaar,

F   Bb   F
Yaaron mohabbat hi to bandagi hai,
        Dm   Gm   Bb   F
Yeh na ho to kya phir bolo yeh zindagi hai,
     BbM7   F   F   Bb
Koi to dilbar ho yaar jisko ho tujhse ho pyaar,
     F   BbM7
Koi to dilbar ho yaar,

Am   Bb   C
Teri har ek buraai pe daante woh dost,
FM7   Bb
Gam ki ho dhoop, to saaya bane,
F
tera woh dost,
Bb   F
Naache bhi woh teri khushi main,

       F   Bb   F
Are Yaaron dosti badi hi haseen hai,
       Dm   Gm   Bb   F
Yeh na ho to kya phir, bolo yeh zindgi hai,
    BbM7   F   F   Bb
Koi to ho raazdaar, be garaj tera ho yaar,
    F   BbM7
Koi to ho raazdaar,

Am   Bb   C
Tan mann kare tum pe fida, mehboob vo,
FM7   Bb   F
Palkon pe jo rakhe tujhe, mehboob vo,
Bb   F
Jiski vafa tere liye ho,

Artist: K.K.
Movie: Rockford
Scale: F Major

Arey Yaron...

Dosti badi hi haseen hain,

Yeh na ho to kya phir,

bolo yeh zindagi hain,

Koi to,

Ho razdaar,

Begaraj,

Tera ho yaar,

Koi to, ho razdaar....

      F   Bb   F
Arey Yaaron mohabbat hi to bandagi hai,
        Dm   Gm   Bb   F
Yeh na ho to kya phir bolo yeh zindagi hai,
     BbM7   F   F   Bb
Koi to dilbar ho yaar jisko ho tujhse ho pyaar,
     F   BbM7
Koi to dilbar ho yaar,

TERE BIN JEENA NAHIN

Artist: Bali Bhrambhat
Album: Tere Bin Jeena Nahi
Scale: D Major

D Bm G A D
Tere bin jeena nahi, o meri jaan-e-wafaa

G A F#m D
Zindagi bhar, saath reh kar, mujhe hona nahi hai judaa X 2
D Bm G A D
Tere bin jeena nahi, O meri jaan-e-wafaa

D G C D
Tu mili toh mujhe mil gayi , zindagi ki har khushi

D Bm G C D
Jism main hoon meri jaan hai tu, bin tere main kuch nahi
Bm G A D
Kahe kya sun zara, aati jaati saanson ki sadaa
D Bm G A D
Tere bin jeena nahi, o meri jaan-e-wafaa

D G C D
Zehn mein mere har ghadi, tera hi khayaal hai

D Bm G C D
Tu nahi toh yeh khushiyan sanam , jaise ik malaal hai
Bm G A D
Aa bhi jaa, aa bhi jaa, sabra ka na le yun imtehan

D Bm G A D
Tere bin jeena nahi, o meri jaan-e-wafaa
G A F#m D
Zindagi bhar, saath reh kar, mujhe hona nahi hai judaa
D Bm G A D
Tere bin jeena nahi, o meri jaan-e-wafaa

Tere Bin,

Jeena Nahi, o meri jaan-e-

Wafaa,

Zindagi bhar,

Saath reh kar,

Mujhe hona nahi hain judaa,

Tere Bin,

Jeena Nahi, o meri jaan-e-

Wafaa....

O SANAM

6

Artist: Lucky Ali
Album: Sunoh
Scale: G Major

G C A D D7 G
Hmm..mm.. Hmm…mm... Ho..o…

G Am
Shaam sawere teri yaadein aati hain
G D
Aake dil ko mere yu tadpati hain
C Am D7 G
O Sanam mohabbat ki kasam,

G Am
Milke bichad na to dastoor ho gaya
G D
Yadoon mein teri main jo door hogaya
C Am D7 G
O Sanam teri yadoon ki kasam

G Am
Samjhe zamaana ke dil he khilona
Em D
Jaana hai ab kya hai dil ka lagana
C D
Nazroon se na yu humko girana
Em G
Mar bhi gaye toh bhul na jaana.

(O Sanam….)

Shaam Sawere teri,

yaadein Aati hai,

Aake dil ko mere,

Yu tadpati hain,

O sanam,

Mohabat ki kasa,.

Hmm…mmm….

G Am
Ankhon mein bassee ho, par door ho kaheen
G D
Dil ke kareeb ho, yeh mujhko hai yakeen
C Am D7 G
O Sanam tere pyar ki kasam.

G C A D D7 G
Hmm mm mm

YE HAWA KEHTI HAI KYA

7

Artist: Aryans
Album: Ye Hawa Kehti hai Kya
Scale: B Major

B **G#m**
(Yeh hawa, kehti hai kya,
E **F#** **B**
Sun to, meri jaana meri jaana) **X2**
B **G#m**
Yeh fizaa, kehti hai kya,
E **F#** **B**
Sun to, meri jaana, meri jaana, Meri jaana....

B **G#m** **E** **G#m**
(Bin tere mai kaise, jee sakunga, jee sakunga
C#m **F#** **B**
tera pyar kab mai, pa sakunga, pa sakunga) **X2**
B **G#m** **E** **F#** **B**
(Meri dua, chahti hai kya, Tera, pyar jaana, meri jaana)
X2
B
Meri jaana

B **G#m** **E** **G#m**
(Mehki hai fizayein, tu kahan hai,
C#m **F#** **B**
Suni waadiyan hai, tu kahan hai) **X2**
B **G#m** **E** **F#** **B**
(Sun le mere, dil ki sada, aaja, meri jaana, meri jaana) **X2**

B **G#m**
Yeh hawa, kehti hai kya,
E **F#** **B**
Sun to, meri jaana meri jaana
B
Meri jaana., Meri jaana, Meri jaana, Meri jaana.

Ye Hawa, Kehti Hai kya,

Sun to , meri jaana,

Meri jaana,

Yeh fizaa, kehti hain kya,

Sun to , meri jaana,

Meri jaana,

Bin tere main kaise,

Jee sakunga,

Tera pyaar kab main,

Paa sakunga..

PURANI JEANS

8

Artist: Ali Header
Album: Sandesha
Scale: C# Major

```
C#
Purani jeans aur guitar,
          F#                        C#
Mohalle ki vo chat, aur mere yaar, vo raaton ko jaagna,
             F#             C#
Subah ghar jaana , kood ke deewar,
            A#m                F#
Vo cigaretee peena , gali mein jaake,
           G#                          C#
Wo karna daanton ko, ghadi ghadi saaf,
           C#
Pahunchna college hamesha late,
         F#                             C#
Vo kehna sir ka , "get out from the class!"

Vo bahar jaake hamsha kehna,
         F#              C#
Yahan ka system, hi hai kharaab,
        A#m                F#
Vo jaake canteen mein, Table bajaake,
        G#                 C#
Vo gaane gaana, Yaaron ke saath,
     C#
Bas yaadein, Yaadein, Yaadein reh jaati hain,
      G#                                           C#
Kuchh chhoti, chhoti, baatein reh jaati hain, bas yaadein..
```

Purani Jeans

Aur Guitar

Mohalle ki vo chat,

Aur mere Yaar,

Aisa yaadon ka mausam chala,

Bhoolta hi nahin, dil mera,

(Purani Jeans...)

```
  C#                          F#
Vo papa ka daantna, vo kehna mummy ka,
           C#
Chhodein ji aap, tumhein to bas nazar aata hain,
        F#         C#
Jahan mein beta, mera hi kharaab,
             A#m               F#
Vo dil mein sochna,  kar ke kuchh dikha dein,
        G#                 C#
Vo karna planning, roz nayi yaar,
```

```
         C#                  F#
Vo khidki se jhaankna, vo likhna letter,
          C#         A#m
Unhein baar baar, vo dena tofe mein,
     F#             G#
Sone ki baaliyan, vo lena doston se,
     C#
Paise  udhaar...,
```

```
  C#         A#m
Ladakpan ka vo pehla pyaar,
        F#              C#
Vo likhna haathon pe A + R,
```

```
C#
Bas yaadein, Yaadein, Yaadein reh jaati hain,
    G#                                            C#
Kuchh chhoti, chhoti, baatein reh jaati hain, bas yaadein..
```